Wrestled From The Raritan

Patrick R. Engel

BookLeaf Publishing

India | USA | UK

Presentation by *BookLeaf Publishing*

Web: www.bookleafpub.com

E-mail: info@bookleafpub.com

ISBN: 9789360947385

First edition 2024

I would like to dedicate this book to Clark Mullener, Robert F. Engel, and Joseph "Old Joe" Rizzi.

Men of their caliber and quality could never be captured in something so finite as words, but it is my hope that their names will live on in these pages for eternity, just as they will live on in my heart and my work henceforward.

ACKNOWLEDGEMENT

I would like to thank the following individuals, in order of their appearance in the story that has been my life:

To my mother, Kelly, who showed me more about being human than any book could have taught me. In your journey, I too have found my direction, and together we have come so far. You taught me that a mistake is never final, and we can always pick ourselves back up again from the coldest, darkest parts of the earth. No matter how far I strayed, you always lifted me up, as if you knew I would one day correct my course. You also taught me to be blunt, with both the ones we love and the ones we don't, and there are few better qualities to have when writing poetry, so I hope you see a part of yourself in these pages, just as there is always a part of you with me each and every day in this crazy world. I love you Ma.

I would like to thank my father, Alan. You always taught me that the easiest path would be the most traveled, and I think it's an understatement to say I took those words to heart. You always have been, and always will be, the first hero in this world I idolized, long before the great tales of Heracles and Odysseus filled my heart with inspiration. May you always know the cherished place you hold in my heart, and the desire I will always embrace to be even half the man that you are. I feel pity for the great men who came before, whose histories we study, that never had the privilege of calling a man like you their father.

I would like to thank my stepmother, Terri, who taught me one of the greatest lessons there is: Love transcends all things in this world, even blood. I have watched it exponentially, in how I see you care for my father and me to this day. I didn't understand until maturity that your purpose in my life's plot was to teach me more about myself than I would have ever known, through both loving support and pressed accountability. It is only in my budding wisdom that I understand this and can truly be thankful for the way in which you have shaped who I am as a person.

To Steven, my dearest friend and cousin, I owe some of my greatest appreciation. There have been many times where I have waylaid the periphery of my own mind's facility, and each time you have been there to ground me. Through you, I have learned how it is possible to love someone so much that you would sacrifice anything for them. The bond we have shared since the day you entered this world is unfathomable and can never be contained by the timid concepts of time and space. You are my greatest friend, but also my most faithful confidant, and without you I am sure I would never have achieved the things I have achieved in this chapter of my life. Seeing you with your beautiful family continues to remind me that there is still so much good in this world, and that we should never give up on encouraging that. May you always know how dear you are to me little cousin, and may we always safeguard each other, in this life and the next, my brother.

To my stepfather, Mario, a man of many words, and few regrets. You always entertained my wild ideas and creative thoughts, and because of that, I have grown to accept my creative self and process more. Without this confidence, I am not sure I would be writing this today, and genuinely appreciating it for all it is worth. You have spent more than a decade dedicated and dutiful to my mother, and for that I can never thank you enough. She has grown in your world, and has become the best version of herself, and this is because pure love will always promote the best well-being of the other individual. You have also extended this supporting love to me, in so many ways, and I cannot begin to explain how much I value the many talks we have had and the times together. As I enter this next journey in my story, I am beyond grateful that it will be one that you had an opportunity to be a part of from the start.

I would like to thank my love, Ameryn, for your unending support and your example as one of the greatest women to have entered my life. I want to thank you for taking me from my deepest pits of despair and dragging me out into the light. When I had nothing, and felt like I'd lost it all, you carried the burden and supported this dream. You worked endlessly to pay our bills, double shifts and extra days, all so I could pursue my writing instead of settling for a job I would loathe. When it all paid off, and I began to make a living off my writing, you asked for nothing in return when you were owed the world. What love is purer than that which comes without expectation of reciprocity? Is that not, in its essence, the truest form of love we can imagine? It must be, I argue, because you truly and wholeheartedly believed in me like I could not. You are indeed the best of what we hope most for humanity: never judging, never bitter, and never cold. When I was always at my worst, my dear, you were always at your absolute best. For that, Ammy, I will always love you.

Lastly, I would like to thank my sweetest girl, my "honey-honeys," my Babygirl. When I look in your eyes, I see all the purity, beauty, and wonder left in this world. Though you will never be able to read this, you were lying right next to me each night I wrote it, so, in a way, this will always be our book, written together. Thank you for what you have taught me about myself, and about the love I can have for another creature. Now you, too, will be immortalized in these pages, so all the world can come back here, read this, and know that you were the very best of all the good girls.

PREFACE

As a kid, I would sit up at night after my parents would go to sleep with a flashlight and I would relentlessly read. What a rebel.

Night after night I would sit there, sneaking this ritual, and losing myself in another literary world. Poe, Grisham, Doyle, Bradbury, I was consuming every book I could get my hands on. Reading was more of a passionate love affair than an escape from reality, and I couldn't get enough. As I started to read more, I started to think of how to expand the stories I was reading. I would imagine how I might create a sequel work or expand on the characters when there really wasn't any further explanation for them in the source material. This mental cataloging of literary plotlines inspired what would become one of my truest passions in writing, while giving me my creative footing.

In conjunction with this newfound love of the written narrative, I was also developing a wildly diverse taste in music as a teenager, and before long the music had also enthralled me like the pages had. Naturally at this age, music and its influences stem directly from those that raise you, and I was fortunate to have a father that still had one of those old CD books lying around. As I flipped through the pages, and saw names like Bruce Springsteen, Bob Seger, Metallica, Fleetwood Mac, Type O Negative, and Marvin Gaye, I was spattered with a fury of different musical tastes and genres in one collection. To this day, I feel as though this might have been one of the most impactful singular moments of my young life. I had discovered a beautiful art form, and lyrical content that vastly contrasted but always spoke to me in some way.

As the summers and winters went on in New Jersey, my father and I would occasionally drive to vacation in upstate New York. We would listen to Springsteen, or Zeppelin, and he would tell me the stories of each band, album, and even song. I was being schooled directly, and the memory of seeing the light flare in my father's eyes as he told me more and more about each new track still brings a smile to my face. His passion, his love, was pouring out of him, and he was showing me all of this because he wanted me to have that wonder as well. He was showing me not just the music, but the love of the art and the story behind it. To this day, I think about how these trips and memories shaped my future self, and how they showed me what it meant to truly have a passion for something, the kind of passion that billows from the deepest part of you when stoked.

As these events were commonly unfolding, I was approaching an impact point in my life where both major artistic influences were going to collide, and they were going to do so in the most unexpected way possible. My father told me one day, as I espoused my newfound love of all kinds of music, that I should consider writing songs. I had an admittedly decent ability in writing, and with loads of creative plot lines and thought experiments I had exercised in my habitual reading, I figured it was something that I would take a shot at.

It was a completely groundbreaking moment in my life.

All my attention that was once spent reading was now heavily focused on writing instead. I became lost in the idea of freeing my thoughts onto a page and then passing this love off with an excuse (like saying that I was writing song lyrics) so that I didn't seem like a loser to my "cool" friends. But somewhere in the unsealing caverns of my soul, a deep and eager reverence for poetry was forming. I began to fill notebook after notebook with poetic writings, stuffing front and back covers if I needed to. I started to just write everything down that came into my mind, in the same prose that had appeared. No structure. No rhythm. Just blatant honesty, like a faucet streaming out of my mind. I began varying in style, in prose, and soon I found myself filling even more pages with a fusion of different poetic styles and tones, ultimately experimenting with the art form while assessing the limits of my own introspection.

This truly is the perfection in poetry that so many people seem to miss. It is, in and of itself, a therapeutic art form, often rooted in self-reflection. It does not bind you by rules set in stone, and it does not tell you what you can and cannot say. As you read this work, you will see that I took strong inspiration from these aspects of poetry, and in doing so I went back to that spectral place, at the fervent discovery of the craft, where I fell in love with the art form long ago.

Throughout the weeks drafting and organizing this book, I experienced an array of life events that deepened my appreciation for this art form. Through loss, love, forgiveness, and gain, I found solace in writing. I channeled much of myself into this work, and I hope that as you read it, you can connect with the sincerity and fervor that I've poured into these pages. This book is not just a collection of poems, but a testament to the transformative power of words and the healing potential of self-expression. I hope that, as you read this work, you take a piece of this with you, and also rekindle those passions you thought long lost to your past.

Their Journey Was Never Yours

Between the aspirations before,
And the spaces in between,
We can only beg to find ourselves,
Amidst something more serene.
A promise in the eventual end,
Gives us hope for bitter retribution,
That the lives we all lived were to mend,
A broken part incapable of resolution.

In hellish and harrowing times,
We cling to the gasps of our past,
Screams from the silence within us,
A task for us to master at last.
Challenging into a new form,
From loneliness and the disorder,
Of sickly times here before,
Now the suffering is so much shorter.

We learn to grow within and outside,
Of comfort and discomfort alike,
Then we brag about surviving to our friends,
And beg them to spend with us the night.
I see it from here and to nowhere,
A long journey going alone,
Starting over with a new frame,

And a new setting where we can atone.
Relocating ourselves from in here,
Both in mental and physical ways,
Are the sources of how we can now grow,
And develop a new sense of acclaim.
Dying miles from where you were born,
Is no way to live on the edge,
Unless it's the ridge of happiness,
And you've no urge to explore 'til you're dead.

The changes will start with you first,
In the heart of your mindset and soul,
Push it to be who you want here,
And never pay anyone's toll.
You will fall and you will regret it,
Getting up and ever trying that thing,
But dust yourself off and be proud now,
No one ever won by saying no to the dream.

I know you will sit there and think soon,
"I can't do this, I don't have it in me,"
But Rome wasn't built in day, girl,
And you know that's my favorite city.
Step out and down onto new ground,
Either here or far off away,
Give yourself the support that you would need,
If you received it in some other way.

Like water cracks the hardest of limestone,
The shame will slowly flake off,
Carried away in the water,
Of happier and more supportive thoughts.
A purpose is all that you're needing,
You tell me this every day,
You forget that your purpose is to think clear,
And never let yourself get in the way.
Keep trekking on this and all journeys,
No matter where the stars decide to guide you,
I'll be here at home with the light on,
Just waiting for you to come through.

In The Winter, I Found You

The reflection,
On the shoreline,
Is reminiscent,
Of the purified.
Have we not had,
A chance to see it?
The days are gleaming,
And lacking torment.

We have gone out,
To the winter trail.
Lost and lonely,
We wandered there.
Love's cold longing,
Left us bare,
Too warm to die,
Too cold to share.

But then we came upon,
Each other shivering slightly,
Begging for the sun,
Embracing each other tightly.
And at that time in bond,
We looked into the other,
We realized we could both go,
We didn't need any others.

So out I reached my hand,
You grabbed it like a rail,
We looked ahead together,
Our ship had now set sail.

No matter where we may walk,
On this earth or in the next,
Like shadows I will always bind to you,
Like fated magnetic objects.
Had I eyes like Oedipus,
Near you, I would still know,
Your beauty is immersive,
It allows my heart to flow.
As we nervously enter,
The next phase from the one past,
I will always feel you with me,
And love you like every day is my last.

NYC '11

Burning out of Jersey,
Any way we could get across,
Breathing the air like it was different,
Always willing to take a loss.
I wandered the streets,
In my twenties' haze,
Chasing my juvenile dreams,
And stumbling through her intrepid maze.

The shattered and freckled girl,
With red hair and bloodshot eyes,
Within her laughter, an echo of pain,
Those suffocated northeastern skies.
We'd meet at those dim lit stops,
And her favorite old shitty dives,
Trading looks, and shooting vodka,
Exquisitely telling each other lies.
The subway jarred our bones,
A hungry rhythm forever in our veins,
As we rode uptown and down,
Our inhibitions were now unchained,
Her tattered dress flicked freely,
No worse than anything else that she'd worn,
We were rebels,
With no philosophy,
Or maybe poets,

Within monotony,
We were an aura of wandering souls reborn.

The city, we all knew, whispered,
Its secluded and storied tales,
Graffitied walls and payphone calls,
And sometimes a few smoking trails,
Indie bands blaring loudly,
From crackled amps in smoky basements,
Warehouse raves in abandoned buildings,
You'd always fret over your college placements.

Gazing at the bridge from the rooftops,
Dumbasses on our friend's fire escapes.
Remember the time that you pushed me,
And then cried at the look on my face?
The skyline was always a canvas,
For our barren dreams and thrilling desires,
Believing that we were great dreamers,
Instead of punch-drunk, co-dependent liars.
Long nights were most often bled,
Into discreet, hungover mornings,
Sublime moments that were etched,
Or recalled as a future friend's warning.
We were young, and wondrously reckless,
We lived as if we were divine and invincible,
In the city's enveloping, brutal embrace,
Everything wrong seemed so damn fixable.
Now, all these years later,
I close my eyes and I can barely reminisce,

Those hopeless, beautiful nights in the city,
Memories of my youth, running amiss.

After Everything, This Is How It Ends?

In the grit of actuality,
Dredging through hallways enshrouded in dark,
Living was nothing more than a gift,
Love was nothing more than a spark,
A fleeting desert's mirage,
A contrast so stark,
Showing me who I was,
in the world's unforgiving dark.
Your eyes, deep coastal inlets,
A siren, tying me within,
In your irresistible charm,
Living felt like a forbidden sin.

Time, though, a ruthless tyrant,
Conducted the fate of our heart,
The enticer of fate once again,
Knew how to play their cruel part,
They carved gaping chasms,
In our broken little hearts.
Left us colder to each other,
And each, alone, wandering through the dark.

Your cherished laughter,
Became a ballad,
As your touch,

Was an empty space,
Every moment became, together,
A memory's frosted and weakened embrace.
Just as roses can't help but wither,
So, too, did our love,
Once soaring like an eagle,
now a wounded, dying dove.
Words, sharp as daggers,
marked love's final breath,
In the grand theater of life,
We learned of love's silent,
Unnoticed death.

Left Beside It

When you're there,
On the edge of it all,
Look back,
And take my grasp.
When you are isolated on the brink,
Give me a stop,
A quick moment,
To beg you to look away.
Nobody is ever going to love you,
Like I need to,
Here in this locus,
And across every looming space.

We are of one now,
And forever conquered now,
The awareness,
That we are the best of each other,
And in each of the other,
We see the future again.
A sight we have not seen in so long,
And it is here with us at very last.

Curse the distances of Hell that split us open,
The distances apart,
To be vehemently broken.
They cannot contain me, or us, or they,

They cannot strip this deluged want from my
needless soul.

And for that, though, of course,
They will only try to make it so.
But I will never let them.
They will never take the ember of frenzy that
exists,
That exists solely in the spirit of tenderness.
A lust,
Defined not by those in it,
But instead by those left beside it.

And of the inferiority in all others,
To stare at you, to see your eyes.
Like the Medusa they turn to stone,
They are not worthy.

The fire of loving you immolates me,
Eclipsed only by the idea,
Of having your love in reciprocity.
I am weak for you, here,
In slicing pieces of it,
Understanding the value in a heart,
But seeing no value in any other than you.
Seeing no light in any but you, like the Sun to the
surface.
Seeing no fear in you, as the son in the arms of
mother.

Seeing nothing, but you, and the privilege to exalt
you,
To carry in myself the knowledge that,
Even across the quantum,
You are the mechanism that drives me,
You are the bridle that I yearn for,
Because in you, through you,
All the things in the world that weigh you,
They are immeasurable,
against the unfathomable mass,
that is the gravity of your fidelity,
in soul with me.

My, how the heavens,
How the heavens open,
And sneer in jealousy,
At the truest essences of your soul, my love.
The beauty of it,
Still leaves me gasping,
And suffocated,
Needing you as you are,
And begging in humility,
For the day I met you.

Flaying Eros

Smoke billows out of the tiny crevice,
Dim light shines across her face,
While the air is sucked out of the room,
And my spine contorts out of place.

Wind whipping against the windowpane,
Growing restless in its night.
Pressing into our conversation,
Like a stubborn butter knife.

The line of light cuts into view,
Above your nose it rests askew,
As you yell and cry and beg,
For the bond that's now reneged.

And in the distance, we see a view,
Timid, yet telling that it's new,
For whence we once did walk,
Did never, truly, ever we talk,
Or gaze upon its crest,
The face that we have seen,
A million times or more,
Or somewhere in between.

But back again to you,
In all your burning sorrow,

Now bending on a knee,
Now pleading for tomorrow.
The pain you feel will pass,
But sudden is its grasp,
No longer will you be mine,
Memories and places left behind.
To litter across the future,
And fill a distinct humor,
To elevate the days,
Thinking in new ways.
You'll love yourself again,
A noble quest herein,
For a person to repent,
Forgiven, like time spent.

You will find yourself a place,
In the end, though, maybe alone,
Where you can initiate, replace,
A place you once could call your home.

Dualities Hominem

The people that we realize,
Are the ones who put us here,
Along with those that raised us,
Sometimes with worried fear.

But when you get unfolded,
In your mind instead of years,
You will see that they are human,
They have dreams and they have fears.

Imagine being tasked,
With the hardest job on earth,
To take a human life,
And raise them real, and true with worth.

For eons we have tried,
To term virtuous thought,
To ask all the inquiries,
And pass on what we are taught.

They took this chance with us,
And did remarkably,
They took us into their lives,
Disrupting, of course, were we.
The courage it must take,
To love one without fault,

To see them as a future,
In time and space, in all.

To hold something so fragile,
And feel this powerful way,
The duality of a person,
The best that humanity displays,

Through all of your futility,
They will weather, and wither, and cry,
They will hope for the greatest out of you,
And you'll let them down most of the time.
But then the day will come,
Where you got it, you figured it out,
You cracked the code of the enigma,
And your head is above and about.

Guess where they will be in this moment,
When you're at your best in your joy?
They will be right there, smiling right at you,
More supportive than Achilles at Troy.

Yes, those humans I mentioned,
They are stronger than you or I know,
They are also the people I know now,
Who would never really let me go.

To them, if they are reading this today,
Just know that I realize it now.

Just how incredible you all were,
Raising me up from the ground.

Our Faces

To think,
Every person you see,
Eyes their own version,
Of whom you are, ultimately.
What we imagine,
And what we propose,
We look like to ourselves,
Only we will ever know.
What we put on when we leave,
And we go about our common forays,
Is a mask we dramatically weave,
"Who do I feel like being, nowadays?"
Whether we are carrying with six,
Or pissing in the street,
The mask is one of our tricks,
The game we play, to compete.
So, while we see what we want,
Others see as they desire,
Why are we so concerned,
With masking ourselves like honest liars?

St. Matt's Fair

Trying to disappear without a trace,
At the fair, we found our place.
Dim lights and laughter in the air,
Mixing liquor without a care.
Beneath the canopy's rise,
We found an excuse buried under lies.
In the pull of the night we aligned.
Those late summers, forever in my mind.

But seasons change, and time moves on,
The echo of songs and summers gone.
Yet in the heart of this aging town,
I feel those memories running abound.
So I walk down the familiar streets,
Where past and present, in reflection, meet.
The laughter echoes, a yearning sound,
In the empty lot where my fears were drowned.

And as I stand here, sky above,
I'm filled with gratitude for that summer love.
Here's to the nights that we won't forget,
To the summer love and the sunset.
St. Matt's fair, in your lights I see,
The best of times had escaped from me.
Though the fair's quiet, and the crowd is gone,
The magic of youth is never withdrawn.

So here's to the memories, bittersweet and bright,
To St. Matt's fair, and timeless teenage nights.

A Toxicity in Magnetism

I miss you like the feeling,
I had when I left it all behind.
I miss you like the days we wasted,
and we can no longer redesign.

I will shatter my serrated soul,
And cripple under the weight,
Battle the darkness forever,
A massacre of alleged fate.

I would love you from now,
To the distant ends of your earth,
Whether through hell, through torment,
Through my own visceral rebirth.

I dream of you like the moon,
Must beg the night for the sun,
Like the sand must beg of the rain,
Like the barren must beg for a son.

Crawling across and tearing,
Pulling myself along,
Through sufferer's perseverance,
I'll be there one night before long.

Tear the flesh from my back,
And upon it I will carry,
Your hopes, your dreams,
The pain is only arbitrary.

Like Orpheus at the mouth,
I cannot help myself,
From looking back to you,
From offering my help,
And for that I will suffer,
Just as he did years ago then,
But as you know I am weaker,
Than the heroic Mycenaean.

The heat of Hera melts away,
And the earth is hoist high,
The flesh strips from my skin,
As the sacrifice is nigh.
I give it all for you,
For the bouts and the fury,
Because in the end for me,
I am only a dreamer on your jury.

Chasms

Fracturing around us,
We cannot see the signs until they are gone.
We are the ones we trust to hold it,
But we have broken it apart before too long.
I see the chasm opening wide,
And the fear we once knew consuming.
Pulling us into its icy grasp,
In the desert of our own entombing.

A bond we imagined,
Was once more than steel,
Has withered away,
And has left us all to reel,
At the thoughts of each other,
And motivations alive,
We've lost all ambition,
To retain this devotion to strive.

Wringing and writhing,
The snakes are at the gate,
Crawling into the courtyard,
No intention to ever placate.
We see them about and know,
They are a part of our growth,
To see if we will falter,
Or stay down to earth.

The tests that the others,
Will give to us each,
Will determine the many ways,
Our values to go on and teach.
Keep it strong in your days,
Of tempting fortunes glare,
And know that no matter the bearing,
I will follow you anywhere.

Requisite Fortuity

Do you believe that there is a God,
Yet the human condition is so divinely sarcastic?
Does it not reek of the intention of man?
Are we not the greatest of triumphs,
And also, the saddest of failures,
Simultaneously?

Did we create it with earnest enjoyment?
Or did we extenuate the decrepit?
Or was it true, and we're all hopeless then,
Or which one is even right?
I think all, or a bit of some.
But I don't matter to the 'all' of it.

Do we make an excuse in randomness,
Brutal randomness,
That we afflict ourselves to deny the reality,
That God, that if he is here,
Must be more human than we are godly?

Do we ignore it all,
The harsh realization,
And find comfort in the randomness?
In the innocence of arbitrariness,
And the lack of intention in happenstance?
These elements comfort us, right, at last?

Morality is certainly random,
Because intention contradicts the dutiful,
And the naturally effectual,
When in reality,
We just don't want to conceive,
That God may be more like us,
Than we ever wanted to believe.

But who is worse in the end,
You or me, contesting,
Whether attendance or connection,
Matters most with this divine wager.
Maybe this, I say it is so,
That you do what you want if it's right,
But you keep it just that,
Yours, and your business alone.

Accept the random
and the love,
In the universe,
With, or without,
creator, deity, or home,
and I can assure you,
no matter the answer,
if you do this and hear it today,
you'll never feel painfully alone,
than you would have been feeling anyway.

Hypocrisy

Give yourself away, again of course,
For you don't know any of the hurt around you.
You make the decisions to end the rituals of
feeling,
But you feel like only you can act impromptu.
The choices and feelings of your day are all void,
Because the way you could show them yourself
frightens,
And the feeling of pressure from outside reserves,
Is akin to a noose as it tightens.

You have made it a show, this pain and this hurt,
Because you know that you are always the
righteous,
Any word that is uttered, at all, in all ways,
Is a chance for your high court to indict us.
In love with yourself above all others,
Yet you hate yourself enough to rebound truth.
You hate the parts of yourself seen through those
others,
And you fight all those people nail and tooth.

Looking into yourself,
Is the hardest imaginable test,
Of the person that we claim to be,

And, of this, I know you detest.
Push yourself into something,
That will help you see the ways,
That you have tainted a new following,
And changed the rest of your days.

Some things can be said,
And can be undone at the easiest request,
But with what you have done to the sanctity,
Face yourself, at last, at your behest.

Desert Lighthouse

So go along now,
Keep her safe there,
She doesn't realize,
How much you must care.

Keep her in light,
Not callous darkness,
Don't ever look back,
Or you'll have lost it.

Keep the focus,
On the impending,
Where you have seen,
The sorrow ending.

Use her visage,
As a beacon,
And see her always,
She'll never weaken.

Her blinding soul,
Will lead your way,
Slitting time,
And twisting space.
She is always,
The best of us,

And the rest,
Of the hope we trust.

Why Am I Here If I Can't See?

Isolation, Reliance,
Elation, Defiance.
Unfathomable, I know,
The stains of the mind in which we live.
Make it seem impossible to grow.

Concealing ourselves,
by masking our disdain,
In the bitter end though,
We can't help but beg,
Beg,
And beg,
For all of it,
All of it, over and over again.

'So, what is the point?'
You ask of a friend.
Are we here for a reason?
Are we truly made of sin?
"No," we must admit,
You have it all wrong,
Life is only meant to be,
A game for the weakest of the strong.

And when you figure it out,

They will tear you down because of it,
When they see you want to change it,
They will disassemble your recognizance.

There really isn't a purpose,
To life and living, that is clear,
So, if we have no reason to be here,
Then why, exactly, do we fear?

This is why you must look past it,
The fear and the sweating of mind,
The art is on the walls around us,
Yet we are all helplessly blind.

Find silence and peace in the stringent,
Or the lazy of your worst old way,
But the meaning of our whole existence,
Won't be found on a singular day.

Read what you can and the authors,
That pretentious assholes claim they read,
But I guess at the end of the world,
All those assholes, and their authors, will all be
dead.

Do you see why it doesn't really matter?
And that, right now, that's not all too bad?
Do you see that we usually ignore the latter,
And look at the invalidating instead?

Malheur County

Summer shimmering across your skin,
A striking canvas of supple silk,
Flowing hair against the headrest,
Complexion fairer than ambrosian milk.
The Oregon hills in the back frame,
Scoring the scene like a composer,
Springsteen blaring on the stereo,
Playing "Backstreets" over and over.
Those moments with you,
A fated gift for the ages,
And the way I remember your laughter,
In the earliest of love's incendiary stages.
You gave me what I often,
Denied to my own foolish self,
A love that was built on adoration,
Stronger as the clock ticks away on the shelf.

I cherish every second that passes,
Because I have them, always, with you.
Selfish as this is for me to say,
I couldn't say anything more true.

Loving you has transcended the feelings,
That held me back from feeling free before.

Unbound you have left me sincerely,
In my dimmest of times, you were there,
And for that I'll always devote myself,
To you and your deserved due share.
And one day when we are all shriveled,
From the curses of time and our fate,
I'll look to you like I did then,
Cherishing the sun on that same pretty face.

Erosion on the Banks of "Then"

I looked across the river today,
And all I could see was the fading.
The crushing pain underneath the trees,
a symphony of timid suffocation.

I kicked along the rocks,
A decision or commiserating,
Is it harder to love yourself,
or to see yourself as decaying?

I can't give you any advice here,
I also don't know what to do.
I know all you want is answers and truths,
but I can't even be honest with you.

I simply have way too much to lose.

When you feel it slipping away,
and you grasp at the sand,
Maybe it will stay together,
Maybe it won't fall through your hand.

But it always does, doesn't it,
It always falls away to shit.
So, Enjoy this fucked up life,

Just enjoy something, for once,
for a little bit.

Gazing Into The Rain

Without our solace,
We can't see the rain glisten across the skin.
It is a construct,
Both of foreign nature, and our desire to win.
A complex fraught emotion,
Pulling on the fibers of everyone we once knew,
Until the fabric is extended,
A caretaker of love, something we know cannot be
true.

You cannot run from this,
The horrid and chilling feelings of aching.
Always in the wrong room,
Like stumbling in and now haplessly faking.
The sheerly genuine,
They almost always evade our troubled
perspective,
We see them here and there,
And ignore the very thoughts that were once
objective.

Into another, a tremor's subway,
An internal tearing at the framework's substrate.
Collapsing into the other airwave,
And always beating down the urge to sedate.
Sedate a parading desire,

To dig into the part of ourselves we cannot deny,
The parts we know sometimes,
When we aren't too busy writing "can't" instead of
"why."
The beauty in the rain,
Is that in its absence is the promise of sun,
If we tell ourselves the same,
No matter the pressure, we will never be done.

In the end of it all,
Is it the fight, or the cause that burns hottest?
We need the fight to know we're alive,
And the cause to remember we are honest.
Walk out from under the awning,
See it for what it is when the universe leans in,
And feel it hit your skin,
Then look up to the sky, soaking in everything.
Forget the incessant bullshit,
Of your borrowed and menial existence,
And open yourselves to,
The idea of giving yourself less resistance.

Babygirl

In your eyes,
The deepest parts of myself rest alone.
They are in peace.
They are in a place that knows they are loved.
I hope you know,
Altogether and totally,
That this is the world I wish for you.

Though the years may be short,
The time we have here,
Is something that even the greatest of the gods,
Could not take from our grasp.
I see you as the purest,
Of the world's greatest friends,
Whose intentions never waver,
And never falter to feel the love.
You remind me to care,
For the world and the words and the seasons,
And all I ever did to deserve it,
Was to bring you home with me.

Beautiful girl,
An incredible ally,
Our worlds have become one,
Across time and space,
Of the vast cosmos,

And the never-ending timeline of life.
What an incredible gift it has been,
To have you here with me,
All these years and all these places,
You have kept me company.

Just know that you were the first,
Before any others after,
Maybe not the smartest,
Or the fastest,
Or the strongest,
Or the one who hated napping.
But you will always be the first,

My sweet Babygirl,
Forever, and ever, hereafter.

Furnishings

A person decided,
Will always be a person at odds,
With the concept of creating narratives,
That create a new sense of awe.
In searching for the meaning,
Experiencing loss,
Missteps are forgiven,
Completion of the arc.

I have finally come here,
To bear and to preach,
Of the motives of the many,
Who feel it's out of reach.
Believe in the fallible,
And the legends of before,
But always be willing,
To adjust your mind's decor.

Vermilion Reverie

I had never expected,
Such a succinct cruelty out of life,
Until I decided wholly,
To commit myself to living it.

It was not the anguish,
Or the time spent that made it abstractly grey,
But instead,
The incessant bickering,
Of life's ambitions and empirical aims.
I have seen enough at this young stage,
To nullify any prior principle,
In the idea that a person has the ability,
To fully transform the essence of their self.
Instead of rectifying who we are as people,
We simply adapt and overcome,
Much,
Oh, often so much,
Like our species was intended to do.

We are not all dreadful though,
Like the woman at the crosswalk tonight,
Wearing colors of vibrant blue,
And depressingly contrasting red.
Blending with the harrowing red,
Of the piercing red light hosteling me.

Telling me to look at her,
Telling me not to ignore it because I'm here.
So, I look into her and through her,
Seeing her as a stranger,
Yet also as a familiar in some way,
Some way that I cannot name,
Like a taste that you cannot place.
But I see her, and for once,
I cannot shy or look away.
Tired is grained into her face.
Begging for the redemption,
Of a stranger satisfying their own soullessness,
By lending their world to another,
In hopes of their own salvation.
And she is there for it absolutely,
And she is a participant in the execution,
Of her only possession left,
That heirloom on the pawn shop counter:
Her dignity.
It is her obligation to her fated predicament.

"Are we always this person,
When we are seen by others?"
I have seen her ghost before,
Its shadow suffocating the light out of frame,
In that horrendously solitary place,
at the red light.
Staring into the adjacent world,
And seeing it there,
Has shown me repeatedly,

A ferocious memento,
That the beauty in a person,
Can so wholly be stripped from them,
In a society that only we could have willed,
So harshly upon ourselves.

If we had known,
Ultimately,
What we would have created,
Then would we have created it,
In the idea that it would have been "good,"
And not just "good enough?"

In the Boiler Room

Measled and agitated,
And annoyed at everything again.

The uselessness of the arguing,
And the repeating of statements,
Will drive even the sanest of men,
Into a pit of desperation.

Stomaching the way,
In which everyone happens to lie,
And seeing all of the ways,
Disingenuous people scurry by,
Their ideas and their passions,
In a world born less of caring.
Born of the hapless pressure,
Of the abyss's unending staring.

The futility of the struggle,
Across arching and escaping gateways,
Creates distortion in the spirit,
And a yearning for the maze.
Give me two more days of peace,
Alone and unfiltered within,
So that I can continue to grow,
And see the world as a presence again.
To see it, all rearing and ugly,

Snarling at serpents delight in the sun,
Another frigid winter is coming,
And soon it will all be undone.

A product of nestling wastefulness,
A moonwalk on top of the Sun,
For today, for tomorrow,
I refuse it…
The urge to hastily run.

Rise

How long will you suffer,
Until you command the will,
And the principle,
To be of your value?
How long will you let your dreams,
Ripen and rot, stinking,
On the vine of your life?
Not long, I do hope.

I was once as you are now,
Small, blind, menial,
And I had enough of myself,
And what I let myself become.
I had to wither inside guiltily,
To evolve and become new.
The acid of regret and fear,
Melting, peeling the flesh from my soul.

Desquamation of the shell,
Shattering your safety to live in full.
Like reaching through razors and glass,
We are calmly declaring the mindset,
That we have no sanity in us,
If we don't believe we're the upset.

How long, as I said,
Here and times before,
Will you wait for the power,
To want you as yours?
Pick up the hammers,
And shatter the glass image,
Forget the shit you felt then,
And the disgust in your visage.
Clutch your pined fingers,
Around the edges of the rail,
Pull yourself up here,
Rectify your avail.

How long will you wait,
Before you ascertain the truth of fortunes,
That serenity, equanimity,
More important than useless, human torment.

Pop Bob

Stoic as Cato and Zeno,
And determined to cross all of hell,
To make what you want for your family,
And the world can go piss down a well.

In your hands and heart there is courage,
But not simply for what you have done,
It's there for your fatherly duty,
I see it always alive in your son.

A man of many words you were not,
But the stories and proverbs abound,
It kills me I couldn't be there for you,
At the end, I wasn't around.
Off making my life all the richer,
For better and better tomorrows,
I know you would have been happiest,
Begging I ignore this sorrow.

So here we are after it all,
I am here, and you, nevermore.
Nevermore to ask me your questions,
Nevermore to show me your world.
I know I assured I would regain,
The composure and the strength to be glad,
But you were sometimes a man who broke rules,

You knew that the good came with the bad.

So, I will keep my chin up as I see you,
In my mind and my pictures alike,
I promise I won't go astray,
And think of you without delight.
Good morning to every new day,
From here on and here out for now,
But I miss you, I admit, I said today,
As I rested my hand on my brow.

A Descending Insight

In the stillness,
The longing is howling,
Shrill, it is deafening.
Like an echo after a specter.

Have I not lost enough?
Down deep it must be,
In the sepulcher of fates,
In shuddering you cannot follow,
But in the end,
I have still lost,
And yet, then again,
What I am now guaranteed to lose,
Enough for a man to say he is lucky.

Lucky to have those to lose,
And to have a world,
That saw me by more than what I knew,
And the things I only dreamt that I could do.
And only the things I said that were kind of true,
With a meaning, lost, but never forgotten,
To you.

Free Fall

Soaring on, inside my psyche,
The words and the notes,
I cannot give into,
What I want to say the most.

We duck and we dodge,
The barrages of this world,
They rise and fall like oceans,
They birth and kill like worms.

We lie first to ourselves,
And to our overbearing guilt,
So bad it has become,
We wrap up in its quilt.
The shame keeps us warm,
And we deny ourselves the fire,
We take every dream we had,
And instead burn it on the pyre.
We see ourselves as worthless,
For the decisions we have made,
But we won't even borrow the gift,
Of mercy in the shade.

We say, of course, we'll call,
But, alas, we know we won't.
Please don't take it wrong,

It's certainly not your fault.

I guess in the end we try,
To produce something from the heart,
To tell you what we're doing,
To tell you our grand thought,
But every time I call,
I don't know what to say,
The words all feel like marbles,
My tongue, just molten clay,
And I see the cursed image,
Of how good I could truly be,
But the loneliness is loftier,
Than a line cast out at sea.

So, I will continue to talk deftly,
And see how proud you can seem,
I already know that you are, though,
The only one I'm letting down,
Anymore,
Is me.

Post-Trauma Clarity

Distraction from the mundane,
And excitement for the future,
Fill my heart with happiness today,
And tomorrow,
And within itself,
A whole new suture.

A stitching of the pain,
And a healing of the wound.
Day after day again,
I have nothing new to report.

For if it was my choice,
I don't think I would change it all again.
But at this point,
I'm happy it's all 'back then,'
Because that time in my life was shit,
And I'm better than that, at last,
And I don't really care anymore,
About looking back into my past.

So, I keep signaling for the future,
And pinching myself awake,
All day and all night,
I'm grateful for what the stars didn't take.
Cynics are often young.

Realists better be old.
At the end of the endless day,
We all just do what we are told.
So don't blame yourself now,
For the troubles of your day,
They've all become irrelevant,
They've all been washed away.

Give yourself a chance,
Forgive yourself, reclaim,
Create a new chapter,
A new act in your own play.
Say goodbye to the ones,
Who left you kneeling in the past,
Some were there for trials,
Some were there for laughs.
Some were there,
To knock you up,
Some were there,
To fill your cup,
But all were there,
And that won't change,
So, forgive yourself,
Today, and every day.

Sonny

I see you,
Every day here,
In the flicker of the autumn,
Or in the way the mountains freshen the air.
The letters that you wrote me,
I read them every day.
Especially when I think of you,
Or when I've lost my way.

Sitting in your van,
At the park on sunny afternoons,
To go back there again,
Almost anything I'd be willing to lose.
Crawling into bed,
In between you two,
Seinfeld reruns playing,
My cherished memories that are you.

Steven is doing so good,
You'd be prouder than ever before,
A family of his own now,
A future so bright is in store.
Mom moved out to Montana,
Even the mountains, they can't hold her,
A spirit she got from her father,
Something learned as I've gotten older.

I feel you with me softly,
In ways I can't even explain.
I look for you when I am driving,
And end up near Story Book Way.
I feel you when I am writing,
In this moment and in the next,
Because I know you'd be proud,
No requisite or needed pretext.

So, one day at last,
When it's all beautifully older,
I know I will see you out there,
And the memories will surely take over.
All I ask, while I'm here,
You get things ready for me.
Hang up our old white porch swing,
And, together, we will sit in the breeze.

Te Ipsum Vince

Opinions of a valued expendable.
Are the only ones here, alive,
Considered most detestable?
Isn't that what we are,
Not really you, or really me,
But aren't we all the worst,
When the worst is all we want to see?

Contradictions in cerebral intentions,
Prove difficult for the honest,
And the hardworking in retention.
Immersion in toil's ascendant promise.
Bonds meant to break will survive,
They will eventually hold fast,
Just long enough for us,
To see their ironic last gasp.

And if we are lucky to outlast them,
And create with us a world,
That is true, inherently lasting,
That is thrown off of the hurled,
Then we have won in the great,
Yet lost also here, in the small,
Because the sacrifice of several,
Doesn't mean the sacrifice isn't at all.
Tortured with auburn hauntings,

Of worlds which could have been,
Yet here we do not see it,
A blooming world, like a brand-new vision.
The sun it is always against us,
But at least we will know where it stands,
On the day it decides to explode,
On the day when this shitty world ends.

We live like we have no worries,
But panicking won't do us any good,
Just do something that you enjoy,
Do something different for you.
It's actually not hard now,
Though I thought it really was,
To look out and see a weird place,
To look out and see what love does.
So just go do what you want.
I mean, seriously, screw what they reckon.
Be pleased with yourself, for once.
They'll only win again if you let them.

To Audition for Humanity

For everywhere you have been,
You will surely reach again,
Everyone you loved so long,
In the end, returns, to mend,
The different bridges of our regret,
And the ways we can't let go,
Of the lives we won't forget,
Or the love we never showed.

Look back on the things that haunt you,
And forget the ways in which you fought them,
Does the story you tell yourself stay true?
Does the way it all happened now contend?
When you look to the sky in anger,
Do you ever consider the fact,
That luck speaks as a stranger,
And our reality breeds a pact?

Tempted are we to omit,
A life some say bleeds slow and gray,
But we rarely ever see it,
We just get lost along the fray.

We see it in pain and heartbreak,
In fucking, and loss, and love,
But already we see a mistake,

A memory often fits like a glove.
A glove that has stretched and has formed,
To your hand as it has always been,
But add any parts gone before,
And the discomfort can be seen.

So, continue in jovial merriment,
At the thought of your hapless times,
Because we are all just free actors,
And we write almost all our lines.
We produce whatever we conceive,
And forget the costs incurred,
Just to tell others it's free,
Told the way we all preferred.

And when we hit the stage,
And look out at the crowd,
Let's hope they see our age,
And applaud so clear and loud.
Can we fool them with our masks,
That we wear for them, and today?
Can we ignore the pressing tasks,
Maskless… expressionless… in every way.

Thoughts From That Same Park Bench

I see them there, trapped,
Like animals.
Scurrying their way out of a hole that they made
for themselves.
And realizing this will be their finality.

They can't help but feel like the one place that
they belong,
Is also the one place that keeps slaughtering them.
Into a most ragged,
and brutal version of themselves.
It's not a state or even a region,
But instead, a mindset,
That brutalizes the freedoms and humanity,
That the human race was supposed to have driven
into them.

Before the depths of our own greed overcame us.

It's a place that we could imagine going back to,
If we could imagine ourselves being able to act
whole again,
As if we were one person and not an alienated
group of factions.
Is it a utopian concept,

Or is it just a symptom of a daydream,
Considering dreams will always be lies.
Spiteful ones that we tell ourselves,
That we would imagine could come true,
In a world of our own creation.

I find myself dreaming less and less,
Night to night,
Saving those precious moments for the daytime
When I am awake,
For what is the point of dreaming,
If you can't even remember the passions
You lied to yourself about the night before?

Circling the drain of existence
Has never been something we've been good at,
And though we continue to put ourselves in the
bowl,
We always find a way to claw back out to the
surface,
If anything, just to breathe one more gasp of air,
Before plunging into the depths of our own
resilience and sanity.

This is not a testament,
To the depressingly insane status of life,
That we decide to impart upon ourselves.
But instead, a nod to the way we once were,
Not just as a people,
But as a species,

Creating and growing towards a common goal,
And not societal dominance.

We have become slaves to the machines we create,
And then we make slaves of the men and women
Who warn us of these perils,
Dousing them with the shame of
non-consumerism,
And calling them a threat to everything that we
hold dear.
But what is it that we actually hold dear?

Do we hold the concept of what you should be,
Dearer than the practice of who we are?
The answers are not mine to give,
But I feel that by the time I am able to realize
them,
It will be too late to impress them upon another,
And the most cyclical contradiction of the human
condition,
Will become awfully apparent once again,
Just as you and me,
Understand it all in a daydream,
Many years from now,
And many lifetimes away.
Old and gray, we will get it.
We will maybe, finally, get it.

Desperation in Dedication

Life isn't guaranteed,
And boring is death.
Live life for nothing,
Die with regrets.

People have gone by,
Miss them no less,
But people that tried,
One will never forget.

And there you walk by,
Couldn't even care less,
I can't disagree,
I'll die again with regrets.
But none come close,
To how she believes,
In me, in love,
In wanting to be set free.

I fight against my mind,
My body and my spirit,
I fight the urge to rhyme,
Dying to desperately feel it.
At the end of the whittled day,
And the end of my ragged line,
All that I will want,

Is for you to want to be mine.

Do I have that though?
Did you say I have her love?
What else is there anyway,
But an endless sky above?
I'll die with some regrets,
I know that this is true,
But also, of this I know,
One won't ever be you.

Death is the end,
Of life as we know it,
But life spent with you?
When it's done, I'll have to owe it.
Dedication never ends,
Not mine at the least,
And every day I'll worship,
the soil below your feet.
Crazy I am,
Crazy for you,
And there is nothing, for you,
That I wouldn't shamelessly do.

Sal

You had a sickness I could not save you from.
I knew it, but I couldn't admit it when I needed to.
I have lived without you now for so long,
It seems,
Yet I am still thinking of you every day.
I'm sorry I could not make it there;
I couldn't see them all.
All of them who ruined you, who tarnished you,
The You that I knew, the You that had dreams.
The You that rolled the windows down,
And floored it when we went over the bridge.
The smile on your face in that moment,
With the warm Jersey air in our eyes,
We were truly free, my friend.
I will always remember you in that place.
That is the light I will always see you in.

I miss you so great now,
So much more than I expected.
I love you, as a brother to his own.
In peace, I hope you've rested,
For there are few men that I have met,
Who I feel more deserve it than you kid.
Just be sure that you answer the door,
One day, when I knock like I always did.